TWO BEARS
in the snow

Story by Cathie and David Bell

Pictures by Jan Brychta

Oxford University Press

For Emily

Oxford University Press, Walton Street, Oxford OX2 6DP

Oxford   New York   Toronto
Delhi   Bombay   Calcutta   Madras   Karachi
Petaling Jaya   Singapore   Hong Kong   Tokyo
Nairobi   Dar es Salaam   Cape Town
Melbourne   Auckland

and associated companies in
Berlin   Ibadan

Oxford is a trade mark of Oxford University Press

© Oxford University Press 1990
Printed in Hong Kong

A CIP catalogue record for this book is available from the
British Library.

The Two Bears Books are:

Two Bears at the seaside
Two Bears in the snow
Two Bears at the party
Two Bears go fishing
Two Bears find a pet
Two Bears and the fireworks

One morning Stanley and Winston looked out
of the window. There was snow everywhere.
'Oooh, good!' said Winston. 'Let's make
snowbears today.'

Winston made a big bear just like himself,
and Stanley made a little bear – just like him.

Stanley used a carrot for the nose, a twig for the mouth, and lumps of coal for the eyes. Soon he had finished.

Winston was still busy.
'Why is it taking you so long?' asked Stanley.
'Because my snowbear is much bigger than yours,'
said Winston.

'What shall I do now,' thought Stanley. Then he
smiled to himself. He made a snowball and
threw it at Winston.
It hit Winston on the back of the head.

Winston was angry. He made a snowball
and threw it at Stanley. It hit Stanley
on the cheek.
OUCH!

The bears had a snowball fight. Soon they were
covered in snow!

They were having great fun until Winston
threw a snowball at Stanley's snowbear.
The head fell off!

Stanley was very angry. He made an extra
big snowball and threw it at Winston's snowbear.
An arm fell off!

Then they both threw snowballs at the
snowbears. Soon there were no snowbears
left – just piles of snow.

They jumped on the piles of snow and
laughed and laughed.

Suddenly Winston looked sad. He looked
at the piles of snow.
'Now nobody will know what lovely
snowbears we made,' he said.

'Yes they will! Yes they will!' called
someone. It was the little girl from
next door. 'I took a picture of your
snowbears with my new camera,' she said.

The little girl came to show them the
photographs. The bears liked the picture of
the snow fight but their favourite picture
was of the snowbears.